DEATH AND HEARTBREAK

LEAH MUELLER

Weasel Press

Death and Heartbreak
Leah Mueller

ISBN-13: 978-1-948712-46-0

© 2019 Leah Mueller
Photographs © 2019 Leah Mueller

Weasel Press
Manvel, TX
http://www.weaselpress.com

CONTENTS

To Scott and Gerry, who taught me a bit about death and heartbreak.

DEATH AND HEARTBREAK

Meteorite From Saturn

The objects that strike from
above are always the worst.
Driving my Toyota Corolla down I-5 in a
9 PM Pacific Northwest rainstorm,
a few miles north of Everett.
Raining so hard I can barely see.
Traffic like angry bees
escaping from a damaged nest.
Radio off so I can concentrate.

Suddenly, the heavy crash of impact
so loud the entire car shakes.
At first I think a massive rock has
fallen on the roof, then I
can't think at all. The lights flicker,
or maybe it's just the inner light
that flickers, like it almost decided
to go out, and then changed its mind

and said no, I will stay. A projectile
has fallen directly from the sky,
shattering the windshield. Ripples spread
across the surface, circling from the
point of impact. Rain cascades against
the cracks, swirls in thick oceanic patterns.
The glass remains stubbornly upright, as
wipers continue their steady rhythm.

I can't tell if the surface is cracked
or whether it's just rain. The water is
viscous soup on the windshield,
my wipers are no match.
That object came from the sky. No
nearby overpasses, no looming semis.
If I'd followed my instincts
and gone to the rest area, I would
have avoided the incident. Instead,

a cosmic bullseye on the driver's side
of my car. The goddamned thing
was aiming straight for my face.

I keep driving. The rain stops in downtown Seattle,
and water evaporates from the glass.
Harsh overhead lights shine on the
spider web of cracks. I keep driving.
Construction detour in Tacoma, I must go
three miles out of my way, then
turn around and head the opposite
direction on the interstate. I keep driving.

I pull up in front of my house, emerge from the car,
run my fingers over the cracks, note
the impact point with its two perfect,
concentric rings. The missile was determined
to drill a hole and collapse the windshield,
but the glass and I resisted. I was one
with the glass. We resisted together
and I escaped with what remains
of my life. The windshield is less fortunate,
and will need to be replaced in the morning.

Not as hard as beating cancer,
like my best friend did three years ago,
but still a fuck you to death. I never saw it coming,
wonder whether a meteorite or an airplane bolt
wanted me gone. This seems a fitting end
to an especially difficult winter,
except it is only February. A man
drives over and replaces the windshield,
tells me not to wash the vehicle for at
least two days. I say I don't
care if the car is clean, and pay him
two hundred dollars plus tax.
It seems like a good deal to me.

After the Fire

After the fire I heard your voice,
low and Midwestern: the syllable
bursts of erratic heat, hoarse
cadence musical, familiar.
Years in the Northwest turned my own
words into monotonous rain. Your clumsy
thrust ejects from my belly, illuminates
my breath with manufactured warmth.

Two Decembers ago, we hiked to
Multnomah Falls summit, and
I showed you the river below. Your face
in the wind, pale from Michigan cold.
That sideways look of appraisal.
Your body as it ascended the switchbacks,
liberated from the tyranny
of asphalt and party stores. Both of us
waking up in the Jupiter Hotel,
spent and wanting more. Later,
you shed airport tears, but I refused to stay.

Somewhere along the path,
your hat flew away: its absence
a mystery after our descent. Though
you searched the parking lot, the hat
was already gone, nestled in the brush
like a terrified animal. In the lodge,
you shrugged over a beer and cut
your losses. We drank a toast
to our own impermanence.

Somebody played with firecrackers,

4

evergreens erupted into flames.
Underbrush burned to jagged
cinders: trail closed until further notice.
I wonder if the fire rustled
your hat from its hiding spot, tore
the canvas to shreds. Probably
it remained hidden for as long as it could.
You would know a bit about that.

The waterfall continues its plunge
as I wait for the trail to re-open. I
will your voice into submission, but
your ersatz heart springs from
my chest before I have the chance
to extinguish it. You have the audacity
to light matches during a drought, and I
was never much good with water.

Thoughts and Prayers

My stepfather got a postcard
    from the 700 Club
        a month after his suicide.

The televangelist urged everyone
        to call a toll-free number

            for prayer healing, and
                a free "Jesus First" pin.

He claimed to have a powerful
        and intricate communication system:

gunmetal cables, shooting prayers
        towards the almighty at speeds

            faster than sound or light.

My stepfather lived in rural Illinois, a
        place where prayer was
common as pie. He drove twenty miles to
    buy beer in the next county, free
            from the Church's vigilant eye:

drank his liver to flames,
    body slumped against the couch.

His strap always near, ready
        for punishment. The beating
            worse if you flinched.

6

My stepfather didn't believe
          in guns. He chose fire instead,
                    a dress rehearsal for the Afterlife:

          One morning at sunrise, he
     doused himself with lighter fluid,
        lit the match. His hair burst

                         into flames. The twilight sky
                         radiated with furious burning.

     My stepfather got a postcard
          from the 700 Club
               a month after his suicide

and his widow turned it over
          and over in her hands, wondered
               where the hell the pin was.

Heartbreak Hotel

He bought me a bag
of "Love Me Tender" dog food,
stood in the middle
of the grocery aisle
and imitated Elvis, but poorly.

3:00 AM mini-mart
after bar time, both of us knew
I was going back to his apartment
after he paid the cashier.

I should have stayed home with
the puppy, but I chose to get
drunk with a man
who left me cold as a
Chicago winter. I was that lonely.
We bought more beer
and headed back to his place, drank
and listened to the stereo until I
had to lie down
on his king-sized bed
to stop the room from spinning.

He climbed under the covers,
tried to kiss me, tenderly,
yet I was having none of it.
His relentless hands moved down
the sides of my neck
towards my half-exposed breasts,
but I stopped him abruptly
and burst into noisy tears.

8

"I'm sorry," he said, "I
really like you."
"It wouldn't be right for me
to fuck you," I sobbed.
"I don't have any
feelings for you whatsoever."

I lost consciousness, while
he hovered above me
on the enormous mattress,
staring down at my face
with a tragic expression.
The following morning,

he looked devastated, so I
promised to call after I had a
couple of days to think.
At least he was smart enough
not to believe me.

I grabbed the dog food
and wandered into the warm
April morning. His street
was alive with tulips of
every imaginable color.
I saw tulips in shades I'd
never noticed before: pale blue
and pumpkin orange and brilliant yellow.

The perfect light overwhelmed
me with pain, as I thought how
beautiful everything would
look if only I'd spent the night
with somebody I loved.

Junkyard Skeleton

The human body has

        built-in obsolescence, cheap
parts born to fail.

You drive through forests of nicotine,

            beer, and microwave nachos,

              with failing brakes and bald tires
                    on twenty dollars' worth of gas.

When the car dies, there is

            no trade-in. After a while,
               you can't afford the payments.

A stealthy vehicle

     arrives in the thick of night,

             sinks a hook under your hood

                 and tows you away,
          leaving a dark rectangle

              that used to be your body.

The virtuous will be sold for scrap,
          and live on elsewhere, in pieces.

The weak evaporate, but slowly,
    cling to light until they disappear.

  Survivors visit the junkyard

        four times a year with flowers, stand
in the rain, remembering,

        then exit when the gates
            close for the evening.

Drivers illuminate headlights
    and turn on the radio,

happy for another chance
        to put a few more miles
    on the engine, until
        it's their time to surrender.

You wait, vacant

        and windowless
    for their return.

Mortality

The two worst things
about death are waiting
for it to arrive, and knowing
someone else will find my body.

If I could fail to deteriorate
and finally disappear in a
cartoon flash of light,
it wouldn't be half as bad.

Knowledge of limitation,
compressed into hourly segments,
a circled date on
the calendar of mortality.

Time to get my work done,
since no one else wants any
part of it. Instead,
the random folding of the clock,
the unexpected power loss.

I pretend to know the route
by heart, and the schedule.

Another person will need
to pick up the slack
after I forget. Somehow they'll
manage to remember, and my
husk will crumble like all the
others before it.

The Two Towers

I died twice, before
I stood beside the river.

Rocks piled like a tent: large
at the bottom, gradually
shrinking until the last stone,
precarious tip
balanced at the tower's summit.

Kickstand: standing tall
against the water. Waves arrive
to push the stones downriver.

Nearby, a small tower on
dry land, also stacked
from wide to narrow. The
taller goes first, tumbles
like marbles downstream.

Privileged trees grow far
from the shore, while others
on the edge cling tight despite
gravity. The stones have
given up pretense,
wait patiently to be demolished.

I died twice this winter, from shock
and the need to remain upright.
I never learned how to bow to
the current. The river
continues, despite my denial.
I turn and head back

to the warmth of my small room,
my fire and armchair.
The thin ceiling covers me like water.

Oz Moment

Pay no attention
to the man behind the curtain
frantically maneuvering levers
to avoid detection. The man
only does what is natural
for someone who hides.

He covers himself with
cloth and branches.
He waves his hands in the air,
talking loudly to confuse
listeners. You are the girl who
believed a boy could fly across
the street. You want
to believe the man. His
huge head looms above.
His lips continue moving.

Something always arrives at
the last minute, to pull open
the curtain. The head grows
louder, halts when
it sees nobody's listening.
You demand an explanation.
You will stand guard in front
of the doorway, until your armor
finally disappears. The man
will vanish with the head.

Pay more attention
to the man behind the curtain
next time you're stupid enough

to leave home. If you wander too far,
you won't remember the route.
The man will take his wagon
somewhere else. You'll need
to retrace your steps, until you
find the place where you fell asleep.

Skinny-Dipping in San Diego

Sneaking into the backyard pool,
hours after midnight: your
parents snoring. We set the
alarm for 3 AM,
so we won't sleep
through our planned
transgression. It feels both

dirty and clean, our
adolescent figures slippery
warm: underwater lights
glowing on bodies
liberated from the constraints
of clothing, from parents'
growling obscenities
behind vodka bottles.
Your mother and father in bed

and mine two thousand
miles away, drunk on cheap
malt liquor, crushing the
bull's face on the can while
reaching for another. Our
limbs almost touching

as we sneak peeks in the
dark for naked silhouettes.
Breasts and vaginas
in blue chlorinated soup,
choreographed and flashing
like strobe lights. We surface, laughing.

"Ssssssshhhh," I say,
"somebody might hear."

Yet nobody hears. Their
ears tuned to unconsciousness, a
depth lower than our
bodies: we plummet
to the bottom, scrape the floor
with fingertips. I tell myself
it doesn't matter what happens
after we dry ourselves
and return to the house,

pretending we've been asleep
the entire time. In the morning it
will begin again: your father
reaching for the bottle,
then your mother's hair.
His turn to be naked
as he drags her from the couch.

You plead with me to stay in
California, but I call
home, then fly over mountains
for the first time. We arrived
slowly, by train. I pointed
at the pineapple trees, and
you laughed, told me they
were palm. Now I flee
towards my parents:
my known abuses, in contrast
to your unknown ones.

The Sun XIX

I remember the Sun
like I remember your father.
No-nonsense, unapologetic.
Just doing his job, five
billion years with the same company.

When it was time to turn on the lights,
you didn't argue with him.You
didn't beg for the snooze button.
You got your ass out of bed
and hustled. It was pointless to debate
the man who controlled your hours.

Your father had a flashy side,
kept a stylish haircut and a shiny car
that he washed every weekend.
When he felt benevolent,
he was the nicest guy in the world, but
if you caught him in a foul mood,
he was a tyrant, smoldering long past bedtime.

Sometimes when you sat with him,
the temperature was perfect,
neither hot nor cold. He surprised you
with another slice of pie, as he
praised your brilliance. You begged
for his eternal company, and
waited patiently for his return.
No one else's warmth
could ease your bones to sleep, as
you reclined beside the water.
No one else could speak

the language of dawn and nightfall.

Someday you'll learn to
illuminate the beam
and will have no need of your father.
The lantern burns without apology
in a room of your own design.
It may take a thousand years for you
to comprehend, but when you do your
flame will eclipse the Sun,
and your untrained wings will beat
with fierce joy against the sky.

The Afternoon of Your Cremation

Strip from bone
and evaporate
to wherever
the dried blood goes.

Memories seethe:
your abrupt assault,
your terrified love.

Bulbous digits,
teeth in a sawdust box
embossed with
an Indian's head.
Wishbone and sage.

You always said
I talked too much,
though my voice
never reached very far.

I pretend you were kind,
pretend you wanted our child.

Your father's
heart attack, then yours.

That boy with curls
becomes your son,
left alone while you sleep.

Final Thanksgiving at Tower Lanes

(for Scott)

Across the

slippery bowling lane

in your rented shoes,
you stared down the alley,

watched the pins topple.

Dark back turned,
you raised one foot,
rotated and
hurled another ball.
My camera clicked
as the machine
reset its rows.

You seemed

even quieter than usual.

My husband and I
drank pints of beer,
but you were sober.Seven years
with no alcohol,

but still outdoors
smoking every

fifteen minutes.

You complained

                  of numbness
                        in your left arm,

raised it high
                  one early morning,
but it fell on your bed

              like newspapers.
When your

entire body went numb,
                  eight months later,

I hope you didn't

              feel it either.

Your Girlfriend the Sex Therapist

Your girlfriend the
sex therapist hates
my guts, and the
irony is: she's a
goddamn sex therapist,

but she thinks
sex with you
is better than ever,
when you claim
it's not very good.

You'd rather be
having sex with me.

If this isn't
the biggest cliché
in the annals of love, I
don't know what is.

The story was old the
first time, before we
even existed,
but you've added
your own garbled sentences.

Polyamory is for folks
in their twenties and
thirties: a time when
the sap rises all by
itself, without

people needing to
talk to somebody else
about why it doesn't
rise any more,
or failing that, quit
and start all over again.

Meanwhile:
some poor sap
pays your girlfriend
big bucks
to distribute
sex advice, while

you humble her on
long weekends
with your contempt,
your rage because
she isn't me.

This reveals
everything
I need to know
about you,
your girlfriend,
and psychotherapy.

Michigan Boy 68

It's fun to be
a narcissistic alcoholic
until the cleaver comes down.

You'll know this
soon, even harder
than you knew it before.

Your voice on the phone,
wasted before 2 PM.

I had to decide
between bronchitis
and seasonal depression and
chose the former.

Had to self-medicate.

You're the same,
only different.
Everything goes inside you,
nothing comes out.

Side-eyes search for
a void that stays empty.

I struggle for air,
but your breath
never reaches my lungs.

You laughed, once,
asked if I thought you were

26

beyond redemption,

so corrupt there
was no turning back,
or turning away.

When you sit on your bed,
greasy gray hair
stuffed inside your thrift-store cap,

playing Townes Van Zandt on
your last remaining guitar,
remember how hard
I struggled not to answer.

Tale of Two Poems

The poem is closed for the evening.

The poem has folded its wings and curled its long beak against its breast.

The poem sleeps like a car at the bottom of an ocean.

You do not see the poem until the sun has risen. You'll need to turn the coffeepot back on. The coil grew cold because you overslept, and the coffee will be bitter.

You lift your head from your pillow, while the poem perches on the far end of your bed, staring.

The poem demands to know why you have been ignoring it. The poem wanted to stay awake and caress your thighs until you moaned and climaxed, but you fell asleep instead.

You feel confused because you thought the poem wanted to sleep. This is why you went to bed and extinguished the light, instead of letting the poem have its way with you.

You ask the poem if it is too late. The poem nods. The poem no longer wants anything to do with you. You beg the poem to stick around, but it refuses. It's your own goddamn fault.

You drink a cup of lukewarm coffee. The doorbell rings. You rise from the couch and answer it. A different poem stands on the threshold, holding a small bouquet. It asks if it can come inside. You say sure.

The new poem isn't as glamorous as last night's poem, but it will have to do for now. Last night's poem isn't coming back. You wonder where it went. The new poem sits on the edge of your couch and smiles.

With enough light, the new poem could be beautiful. There is a softness around its cheekbones that comforts you. You could learn even learn to love the new poem. The morning has just begun, and both of you are wide awake.

Ode to a Dying Tree in My Front Yard

The crooked tree bends
from weight of moss, yet
flowers like an aged
man, dressed
in a fancy suit.

Limb remnants seared
after the windstorm
hang jagged,
nubs exposed to the elements.

Still, the blooms,
their instinctive
search for light.

Thousands of blossoms
open wide, continue their
stubborn animation.

As long as roots
draw water from earth,
the tree will display
flowers. Each spring,
new resolve.

The tree slumps
a little more each year.
Its gray bark is covered
with fungus. One day

it will collapse,
but not now. Meanwhile,
I don't know its name.

Café Roka

A desert dessert of
green sorbet
in a small glass cup

while outside
the mountains disappear,
and the turrets
vanish into black.

Unlearning noise
takes time, and you
have less of it
than ever.

The Pluto line
of death and mines
runs underneath the soil,
buried yet moving.

You perch above
the fault line,
spoon poised in mid-air,
try not to fall off
your chair.

Some day you will die here
like your ancestors,

or make a clean
getaway, and be
forgotten in an instant,
like the dust of bones.

Meanwhile the sorbet

rolls down your throat
and keeps you alive for
a while longer,

until the check
finally arrives.

At the Memorial

Afraid to weep, my son carries
his father's ashes in a cardboard box.
As water roils in the distance,
he steps inside a crater
filled with loose gravel,
twists his ankle, crumples to the ground.

We stand above, hands outstretched
while he tosses in agony on the asphalt.
On the shore, beachcombers
climb dead tree branches,
pick their way through slippery rocks.

My son's right knee ripped and swollen, a
jagged hole in his expensive pant leg.

I remember the other times he fell,
how I failed to offer comfort,
how he refused to cry
unless he had an injury.
How terrified he was of pain.
How he worked to clutch his intestines
tight, like a box, to keep it all inside.

The only way he mourns is
through his body:
he writhes and moans,
grief rising into the air like ashes.

"I'll be okay," he says,
lifting the box high, continuing
towards the water. A minute later,

I hold my jacket open to block the wind.
My daughter steps inside the folds,
lights a clump of sage with trembling hands.

Maybe we'll all meet somewhere,
but I'm inclined to doubt it.
I've been disappointed before,
gone to that ledge and found it empty.

In the distance, children leap across rocks,
their voices rising with the waves.

We each take a fistful of ashes,
toss them into the low tide.
Tiny crabs search our soles for food.

I clutch the dust of a man I quit holding
years ago, but finally release,
and return to my car without stumbling.

He left with no forwarding address,
dead finger pointing on the envelope,
mail piled on the floor
of his tiny, subsidized apartment.
Somebody else sleeps
in the bedroom where he died
she's happy for the refuge.

All we know is shelter, then
someone who remains standing
long enough to let us go.

(Can't Get No) Stupefaction

Your exes are all crazy.

The lawyer has a meth-head girlfriend who
wanders around his yard at night, moving
random objects to scare his wife.

The vegetarian yoga teacher, grown soft
and lonely, lives in Alabama,
sends you bad poetry every day.

Your latest ex, in Michigan,
stays wasted until four in the morning,
then sleeps until it's time to go
to his part-time job in a supermarket.

His girlfriend the sex therapist
thinks you're to blame for everything.

You must be crazy, as well.
There's a clinical term for it,
maybe even a cure,
but you're too lazy to change.

Your daughter thinks she's ill
and takes two kinds of medications,
but she's probably
the sanest one in the bunch.

The world is a storm
of inebriated wasps:
political sports and wars
and threats of future wars.

All of them fighting to the death
in an invisible arena,
for no reason, except
they're out of their goddamned minds
and have nothing better to do.
Why should you be any different?
Let your center come unglued.
Nobody will notice.

The roar of your brain will
mesmerize, until you
can no longer pay attention
to anyone, and they
will fade into a curtain of static.

Welcome to amnesia.
What took you so long?

Nyctohylophobia

The chaos of the ordinary lulls me
into slumber. Silence terrifies:
I court noise. Chainsaws

shriek in the distance,
tear into my ears like the ancient needle

of a phonograph stuck on repeat.
Their familiar song plays without end.

Log overflows with parasites,
busy eating death. They devour
crumbling bark mindlessly,
as I emerge every two hours from
underwater dreams. Death

keeps them alive a while longer,
until it's their turn to be eaten.

I buy a doormat with a blue hummingbird
hovering delicately against
a floral background, place it on my stoop
to keep the woods at bay,

stomp my feet carefully to remove
pine needles, but a few of them
cling to my shoes, intent on reclamation.
My home will be forest again.
It is only a matter of time.

The city is more dangerous
by far, yet safer than primeval trees

whose endless branches spread into darkness.

Nobody can tell me
where the trees stop and the road resumes.
I could walk forever
and still fail to find the light.

Open Letter to My Valued Customers

My Esteemed Air bnb Guest:

This is not a goddamned luxury hotel.

I'm not going to bring you a pony
or a box of quilted Kleenex.

Nor will I appear in my pajamas to
cook you a gourmet breakfast.

Please don't steal my only DVD
copy of "The Big Lebowski."

If you break the window shade
the appropriate response
is NOT to wrap it in brown duct tape
and then leave me a bad review.

There is a light switch on the wall
to operate the track lighting
in the living room,
and another beside the front door
for the porch light.

They should be easy to find,
though I suppose
if you're standing in the dark
looking for them,
the task could be harder.

You're staying in a fully stocked condo in
the Mt Baker National Forest,

surrounded by the wonders of nature,
filled with such amenities
as two swimming pools

with adjacent hot tubs and sauna,
a three-story log cabin built in 1887,
a walking trail beside the Nooksack river,
tennis and squash courts,
free gourmet coffee,
and numerous barbeque grills.

$75 a night is a good deal.

Don't complain that you
can see a dumpster
from the living room window
and deduct two stars for value.
What the hell did you expect,
you myopic and privileged prima donna?

If I put a mint on your pillow,'
and showed up naked
to turn down your covers
and give you a back rub,
you'd still find something
to complain about.

I'm going to come to your home
and criticize your furniture.
I'd pay a hundred bucks to do it. Let's
see how you like that, asshole.

Next time, stay at the Motel 6.

Sincerely yours,
The Superhost Owner of Lone Jack #107.

Polaroid Selfie

In the days before cell phones,
folks had to take selfies with Polaroids.

They held the heavy box
in front of their faces, posed and smiled
as their fingers sought the plunger.

Women wore cats-eye glasses,
while children squinted in
oversized swimsuits and cowboy uniforms.
Husbands looked bored and brutish
with their square heads and military haircuts.

After the paper rolled out of the camera,
an image materialized in mere seconds.

Polaroid film was pricey, but cost effective,
because it included developing, which would
have been more expensive
at the local camera shop.

With regular film, you had to
wait for days to view your photographs,
just to find a couple of good ones
that didn't have your thumb over the lens,

or were overexposed, or underexposed,
or the goddamn flash bulb didn't work,
or you had come to the end of the roll

and didn't even know it, so you just
kept snapping photos that went nowhere.

Polaroid was as random as Kodak.

People stood in clusters,
watching as one photo after another
was ejected from the camera,

only to be crumpled and discarded
in the quest for perfect documentation.

My parents refused to buy me a
Polaroid Swinger, claiming it
was overpriced and shoddy, and

forbade me to spend my allowance
on such a pile of garbage.

One day, I found a Swinger
at a yard sale for a dollar
and decided to chance the purchase.

My parents shrugged and said it
was no concern of theirs
how I wasted my hard-earned money.

At home, I loaded the film, posed
in front of the viewfinder against a
backdrop of cornfields.
I bared my teeth for the camera wizard
and depressed the plunger.

A grainy image materialized on the paper.
In the center, a wraith with my face,
its blurred outlines fading into winter sky.

I waited for the edges to sharpen,
but a cheap gray pall remained on

everything, duller than ashes.

After ten minutes, I realized I'd been had.
The photo wasn't going to get any better,
and I had 11 more left on the roll.

I took the Swinger up to my room,
hid it in a drawer under some newspapers.
I didn't know which disappointment was worse:
my shoddy camera, or the knowledge
that my parents were right, as always.

Big Top

The carnival isn't
over, it's closed
for the night. Brooding
on crates, clowns and
ballerinas smoke cigarettes.

The sword-swallower
removes his false teeth
and smiles, mouth
gap wide as Texas.

Scent of stale
cheeseburgers, crushed
paper cup bleeds soda.
Spent testosterone
and yesterday's garbage.

In a booth beside
the Tilt-a-Whirl,
a violently red,
enormous stuffed mouse
waits in the darkness
for somebody
to finally get lucky.

Half of You

When you meet your shadow,
be sure to be friendly.

Make certain your shadow is comfortable.
Ask who it loves and who it hates.

You already know the answers,
but it will twist the narrative and
make up a bogus story.
You will believe the story.

Spend some time in bed with your shadow.

You will want to know how
it presses against your exposed skin,
how it looks when it can't see itself.

In the morning, eat breakfast together.

Observe the shadow
in its bathrobe beside the sink,
backside safely covered.

Ignore the rings under your eyes,
and your half-eaten body.
The shadow has grown to twice its normal size.

Listen to the shadow
when it launches its narrative.

Most will be repeats
of stories you've heard 100 times.

You will nod with agreement.
Its stories are yours, as well.

You will run into the shadow
in the strangest places:

walking towards you on the sidewalk
at a brisk pace, colliding
and claiming it was an accident,
or beside you, on the mattress,

inhaling the same air. Observe its
shallow breath, deepening
as the shadow grows closer to sleep.

You will want to leave the shadow.
It will cling, moss-like,
to your neck and shoulders,
its flavor inside your bloodstream.

After you have told the shadow everything,
it will make its home in your body.
You will give it plenty of room.

Now the shadow is yours to keep. You
will forget everything you know and
move backwards into fugue.

Hitchhiker

Sixty-five miles from Baton Rouge
she stood on the interstate with her thumb
in the air, and a Datsun pickup truck
with Louisiana plates pulled to a stop beside her,
then stood idling on the gravel covered shoulder
of the road, while the driver motioned
for her to come inside.

She climbed into the passenger seat,
carefully, holding a duffel bag, hastily
crammed full of sundresses and
underwear, a spare pair of shoes and
seventy dollars, all the money
she owned. Her boyfriend was still asleep in
their third floor walk-up apartment
in the lower Garden District, passed out on the futon
in the New Orleans heat, eighty degrees
at nine o-clock in the morning
with three quarts of beer in the refrigerator and
a note waiting for him when he awakened.

He would scream and break the furniture, perhaps,
but somehow, she doubted this,
he only did these things when he had an audience.
She pulled her skirt over her knees as
she crouched inside the cab,
but the man noticed, and looked away, asked
her name and where she was going: She said
Texas, and then a bus to Mexico, buses were
a lot cheaper down there
but until then, she had to hitchhike.

He told her it was dangerous,
and she was lucky he had picked her up
instead of some deranged nut,
and if she wrote down his address,
she could send him a postcard
to let him know she had arrived safely.
She scribbled his name and address
on a torn piece of paper from her purse, then
shoved the purse inside her duffel bag, and
zipped them both securely.

He wanted to know things:

Was she a student? Did she like music?
How long had she lived in the South?

She said hadn't been there long
and certainly didn't intend to stay much longer,
she was fleeing from her boyfriend
to see her mother, who lived the life of a boozy
American ex-patriot in San Miguel Allende
in a large house with lots of rooms
she could wander in, while she figured out
what to do next. She was twenty-two
and worked at a waitress job in the Quarter.
When she failed to report for her shift,
her boss would just hire someone else.

After an hour, the driver pulled over
and said he had to take a leak,
and would return shortly, and she watched
as he disappeared into a clump of bushes a
few hundred feet from the shoulder
of the road, and a lull fell over everything

except for the anonymous, metallic thumping
of car wheels as everyone headed to Baton Rouge.

Finally, the man called her name, and
she pushed the door of the truck
against the humid gusts of air
so she could hear him better, and he said he
had found a bird's nest with three eggs,
and she had to see it, because it was perfect.

As she placed one foot in front of the other, he
appeared from behind the bushes,
pressed the blade of a pocketknife against her throat
and pushed her to the ground—
not roughly, but firmly, as if she were a dog
and he was making her kneel to do tricks. He
told her that he wanted her,
and that she should suck him and
all of it would be over fast.

He guided her throat to his penis
with the edge of the knife
and she placed her mouth there in a daze
then stopped, unable to continue.
"Go on," said the man, and he looked around
for a moment, but no one was watching.

The cars continued to hurtle past,
and suddenly she was filled with rage
at herself, for wasting her life,
all twenty-two years of it,
now she was going to bite it next to a highway
in Louisiana, and it wasn't fair.
It couldn't be possible

that all of it had to come to this.

So, without thinking, she bit his penis
as hard as she could, brought her teeth down on
the pulpy flesh, with all the force
of her jaw, because she had heard
that rapists kill their victims
even if they submit, perhaps more often
that way, but she wasn't completely sure
if that was true, or if she had only imagined it.

The amazing thing was, the man
didn't collapse on the ground afterward—
he gained more strength instead,
and towered above her, scowling.
He waved his knife in the air, and said,
"I really should kill you now",
but then he subsided and stood immobile,
staring at his member as if it were
a sick child, and he a concerned parent.

"I'm going now," he said in a soft voice.
"Stay right where you are.
Remember, I can throw knives."

He walked through the brush to his vehicle,
opened the passenger door,
and hurled the woman's duffel bag
into the gravel on the side of the road—
and then, struck by a sudden recollection,
scooped it back up, slammed it into the cab
and drove away with her sundresses
and her underwear and her seventy bucks.

50

She waited until she was certain he was gone,
and wouldn't return, before she
finally crawled out of the bushes
and began to run, even though she had nothing
to do except go back to the highway
and stick her thumb out again.

Left Behind at the Poetry Leaves Exhibit

My poem dangles from a
tree 2500 miles away:
the other side of the continent,
in the state where you live.
Words, wrapped in plastic,
swinging like fish
on the end of a nylon line.

Since you don't own a car,
you promised to take
a series of buses to see my
poem, then wander
across the campus, searching
for a tree with my name on it.

For a moment, you could
pretend I was there,
and the words animated
by my actual body,
rather than two-dimensional,
tied by a third party
to the end of a branch.

But it's too far for you now,
and you don't know
the bus schedule.
Your boss finally gave you
more hours at your job, and
my words are less important
than they used to be.

In case you change your mind,

52

my poem will remain in the tree
until the end of next week,
twisting in wind gusts
while trying its hardest
to attract attention from strangers.

7.4

When the crack appears,
there's no escape plan.

Those canned goods
you stashed won't help you now.
No scientific way of measuring,

no chance to prepare. All the drills
were useless. You are either
caught with your hands on the wheel,
steering your out-of-control vehicle

through falling objects, or else
huddling underneath your table,
praying for the tremors to end.

The smug assurance of objects.
The dust of temporary structures
not built to withstand pressure.

You are dead center, you will
be the first to fall. It will
be a long time before the rebuilding.

Some Tips For the New Silver Sneakers Instructor

Put a group of elders
in a room with a massive tub
filled with rubber balls,
and invite them to play.

They will comply within
seconds, glad for the
break in routine.

Watch them throw
the balls to each other,
while one of the guys
shakes his hips to jazz.

The elders will play
the whole hour
if you let them:
tossing balls
back and forth,
running around
the room in circles.

At the end of the game,
you'll need to tell them
to return the balls
to the container.
They will comply,
but they won't be
happy about it.

When noon comes,
they'll have to return

to being old, and no one
looks forward to that.

The elders will show you their scars,
detail their operations,
recite a long litany of body parts,
removed for one reason or another.

They will thank you
for teaching them yoga.
They will cover
their bodies with hats and
jackets, then leave: stoic,
fortified for traffic.

You'll scoop up the
debris of class,
return everything
to its proper container.
The rubber balls lie inert
in piles, covered
until the next time
the elders come to play.

Pack Rat

The space between
what you say
and what you don't
is stuffed with clutter:

cartons of discarded lies,
and new ones you bought
in bulk, but never used.

Perhaps you should
have a yard sale, and
get rid of some of it:

but you save
the boxes anyway,
in case you
need them later.

Reunion on Sandy Boulevard

Perched on the edge
of the Howard Johnson
airport shuttle van
in my dark red clogs,

I turn my feet sideways,
place them slow motion
on the side panel,
descend into the parking lot.

Cold torrential downpour,
puddles on gray asphalt,
December air fuggy and close.

We waited two years,
and you look different
than I remember: pallid,
anxious, but familiar as shoes.

In an hour, we will try again
to find everything
we did our best to hide.

Afterwards, we'll open the window,
exclaim about the unseasonable
warmth. Four days until

I return to my husband,
and you to the flatlands, defeated.
Meanwhile, my heavy soles:
all I have to keep me upright.

58

You devour a microwaved burrito
from the corner mini-mart,
our small room reeks of toxins.

"You're in Portland now,"
I say. "There's no excuse
for bad food or bad sex,"
but I'm sure you won't remember.

Warning to Literary Posers

Be careful when you try
to publish your poetry
and be on social media
at the same time. Eventually,
every indie writer in
the herd of literary oddballs will
send you a friend request.

For a while you'll feel important
when they publish your work
on their Weebly sites.

Suddenly, one of them
will get pissed off
at the other, for being uncool, or
for having different politics, or
for being insensitive
or for a host of other trumped-up reasons.

(Yes, I said "trumped-up." Fight me).

They will tear into each other
like rabid weasels, and
it will have nothing to do with you.

One of them will decide
it's your fault too, since you're on
the other person's friend list.
They'll block you on Twitter,
and you can forget about ever
submitting to their shitty magazine again.

No one bothered to tell you
what the argument was about.

Mind you, these are sensitive folks
who write poetry,
people too blind to know
who the real enemy is.

It's not me, motherfuckers,
I'm 60 years old and have been out
of high school for 40 years.
You sniveling little tattooed poser
with an MFA in your back pocket,
you don't even know what pain is.
Perhaps you shouldn't be so careful.

The Folly of Numbers

Before the November 8, 2016 election,
I passed 9 "Make America Great Again"
signs on the route between I-5 exit #236
and Glacier, Washington. The signs were
attached to long sticks, protruding from
the ground like middle fingers.

I can't remember which highway is #7 or
#9, but #542 goes all the way
to Mt Baker. 9 signs, in front of
4 different trailers and 5 modest homes,

all of them covered with dirty moss, old
engine parts and overturned chairs.
America's new greatness hadn't
quite made it to Highways #7, #9, or #542.

After the election, I counted only 1 sign,
propped in defiance against the side
of a trailer. It stood there for 17 months.

The owner remained patient.
He believed his country could be restored to
a more civil time when white men ruled,
women kept their mouths shut,
and the working class was strong.

Finally, the sign disappeared, and now
there are 0 on the route between the off-ramp
and Mt Baker. America must be great again.
Some of us just didn't get the memo.

Desert Dare

"I bet you could smuggle heroin
across the border."

> He lay across from me on the mattress
> and smirked, because he already knew
> what my answer would be.

"Just stick it in your vagina.
If the customs guard questions you,
smile and look like a suburban mom.
They'll never suspect anything."

> He'd smuggled heroin himself,
> in a different orifice, back in the 1970s,
> before numerous stints in jail and rehab

"Everyone should try heroin before they die.
It's good for writing poetry
and besides, you'll lose weight."

> He knew people on the other side.
> They were always holding.
> If I wanted, we could leave right away.
> We only needed to drive for
> twenty minutes to
> get to the Arizona/Mexico border.

"Maybe some other time," I said.

> I'd lived forty years without
> intravenous drug use, and
> had no desire to start that evening.

I just wanted to have wild sex
and go to sleep, like a normal couple.

"Shit," he complained.
"You're so middle-class."

Dreaming of William Carlos Williams at a Vietnamese Restaurant

I have devoured
the entire bowl
of tofu vermicelli,
which made
my belly swell
like a thundercloud.

I don't need
forgiveness.
Nobody else
was going to eat it
except me.

The rice noodles dripped
with salty broth,
and the spicy peanuts
exploded between my teeth
like perfect firecrackers.

Neighbor Zen

The man who lives
above my apartment
urinates often,

his streams chiming
like Pacific Northwest rain.

He also drops heavy
objects onto the floor
and curses, repeatedly.

Every few minutes, I hear
his sounds of release,

some easier than others,
reminding me not to hang on too
tightly to anything.

Short History of Bad Relationships

Caught head lice in Mexico
from my brother or sister:
I'm not sure which.
My mother suggested pet shampoo,
but it was ineffective.
My mother suggested a
trip to the ocean,
siblings in the back seat.

For two long weeks,
I pulled bugs from my hair,
held them between
my thumb and forefinger,
and flicked them out
the window of her car.

My sister helped.
We were nitpicking.

Had a one-night stand with a
guy in Isla Mujeres,
a drunk frat boy from Texas.
Perhaps he caught lice, too.
We never spoke again,
so I had no way of knowing.

A hurricane hit the island, and
I contracted dysentery.
I lay in my hotel bed, moaning, until
the winds finally ceased.

Back home in Chicago,

I gave my boyfriend head lice.
I didn't tell him about
the asshole from Texas.

My boyfriend was the jealous type
and prone to sudden violence.
He had to get a Kwell prescription
filled at the corner drugstore.

Later that morning,
I stood in the shower,
scrubbed parasites from my scalp,
watched nits swirl into the drain.
I didn't think about the future,
just the eradication of pests.

Harold Lloyd

Body pressed
against the clock,
hanging by the end
of one hand, again.
Suspended, dangling over
chasm: nothing above
you except broken numbers.

No one hears the dialogue,
your twisted mouth moving,
or notices the comical spasms
of lips, legs flailing
like an insect's.
The ribbon flickers, repeats.
I am the audience.
I have seen the film,
countless times.
I know what happens next.

Rescue is useless,
the cop not far behind.
Each time you discover a surface,
it vanishes under your feet.

Somehow, you climb higher,
even as you fall.
You land, embrace.
Beneath you,
the indifferent traffic
passes without comment.

Suit still pressed, you

saunter off in search of
a rare steak
and a double martini,
to celebrate your survival
in spite of everything.

Glacier

I know we've arrived home
by the pine scent, and you
almost smile as we climb
from the car, say

"It smells so good
here." I agree, notice
how thin your face looks now,
and how your jeans used to be
much fuller. We've had

a severe year, without pause in
the trenches, and I can feel
the strain in your teeth and shoulders:

those shoulders your parents
taught to hide from confrontation.

You need three days
to relax, after countless doses
of forest medicine, administered
one dropper at a time.

At the waterfall,
I have trouble parking the car
and it reminds you of
your other problems, all

the angles you can never reach. Still,

you steer in reverse, into a parking
spot, and we walk uphill

until the road swallows us whole.
We return to our sanctuary.
The previous day, we
climbed much higher, to Artist Point,
followed the switchbacks

and watched two young boys
run downhill through boulders
as if falling was impossible.

We know stumbling
is inevitable, and we walk
gently through rubble, gaze
at blue-plated lakes, shiver
as fall arrives. The glacier recedes,
but the chill moves in harder than ever.

Later, we drink wine, watch
a sixteen year-old movie: two bodies
curled together on a plaid couch beside
the Nooksack. The years
rage by like angry water, and we
fail to pay attention. We must be
taught to remember.

Leah Mueller is an indie writer from Tacoma, Washington. She is the author of two chapbooks and five books. Her most recent book, a collection of short stories entitled *Misguided Behavior, Tales of Poor Life Choice*, was published in 2019 by Montreal's Czykmate Press. Her work appears in Blunderbuss, The Spectacle, Outlook Springs, Crack the Spine, Atticus Review, Your Impossible Voice, and many other magazines and anthologies. She was a featured poet at the 2015 New York Poetry Festival, and a runner-up in the 2012 Wergle Flomp Humor Poetry contest.

www.facebook.com/leahmuellerwriter
www.twitter.com/leahsnapdragon

OTHER TITLES BY LEAH MUELLER

Allergic to Everything

Bastard of a Poet

Beach Dweller Manifesto

Queen of Dorksville

The Underside of the Snake

OTHER TITLES FROM WEASEL PRESS

Pan's Saxophone by Jonel Abellanosa
Hyper-Real Reboots by Sudeep Adhikari
despair is a mandelbrot set by Sudeep Adhikari
Wayward Realm by Sendokidu Adomi
Ghost Train by Matt Borczon
To Burn in Torturous Algorithms by Heath Brougher
Klonopin Meets Sisyphus by Adam Levon Brown
The House of Eros by Matthew David Campbell
Harmonious Anarchy by Matthew David Campbell
H A I L by Stanford Cheung
Still Life Over Coffee by Robert Cone
The Madness of Empty Spaces by David E. Cowen
The Seven Yards of Sorrow by David E. Cowen
Bleeding Saffron by David E. Cowen
Face Down in the Leaves by Dwale
Wine Country by Robin Wyatt Dunn
Smash & Grab Poems by Ryan Quinn Flanagan
In Winter's Dreams We Wake by Ryan Quinn Flanagan
If the Hero of Time was Black by Ashley Harris
Dormant Volcano by Ken Jones
Email Epistles by Ken Jones
Evergreen by Sarah Frances Moran
I Am A Terrorist by Sarah Frances Moran
Blame it On the Texas Sky by Max Mundan
I'll Only Write Poems for You by Max Mundan
Rising from the Ashes by Meghan O'Hern
Lipstick Stained Masculinity by Mason O'Hern
Chaos Songs by Scott Thomas Outlar
Kisses and Kickflips by Kacey Pinkerton
In Another Life, Maybe by Michael Prihoda
the first breath you take after giving up by Michael Prihoda
the same that happened yesterday by Michael Prihoda
Beneath this Planetarium by Michael Prihoda
Years without Room by Michael Prihoda
Toast is Just Bread that Put Up A Fight by Emily Ramser
I forgot How To Write When They Diagnosed Me by Emily Ramser

Conjuring Her by Emily Ramser
UHAUL: A Collection of Lesbian Love Poems by Emily Ramser
The Escape by Rayah
Taste & See by Neil S. Reddy
Inevitable by Amy L. Sasser
Satan's Sweethearts by Marge Simon and Mary Turzillo
We Don't Make It Out Alive by Weasel
Cut the Loss by Weasel
Colliding with Orion by Chris Wise
Cuentos de Amor by Z.M. Wise
Wolf: An Epic and Other Poems by Z.M. Wise
Kosmish and the Horned Ones by Z.M. Wise
Ghostly Pornographers by Thomas White